Class 66/5/6/9

MARK V. PIKE

Key Books

BRITAIN'S RAILWAYS SERIES, VOLUME 39

Back cover image: 66552 *Maltby Raider* and 66503 *The Railway Magazine* approaching Cholsey station on the Great Western Main Line with 4L31, the 09.03 Bristol Freightliner Terminal to Felixstowe service. 12 October 2012.

Title page image: 66528 *Madge Elliot MBE – Borders Railway Opening 2015* is awaiting its next duty at Westbury. 12 February 2020.

Contents page image: 66623 is seen at Rugby station waiting to head south. 20 September 2007.

Published by Key Books
An imprint of Key Publishing Ltd
PO Box 100
Stamford
Lincs PE9 1XQ

www.keypublishing.com

The right of Mark V. Pike to be identified as the author of this book has been asserted in accordance with the Copyright, Designs and Patents Act 1988 Sections 77 and 78.

Copyright © Mark V. Pike, 2022

ISBN 978 1 80282 246 5

All rights reserved. Reproduction in whole or in part in any form whatsoever or by any means is strictly prohibited without the prior permission of the Publisher.

Typeset by SJmagic DESIGN SERVICES, India.

Contents

Introduction 4

Chapter 1   Class 66/5 5

Chapter 2   Class 66/6 61

Chapter 3   Class 66/9 80

Introduction

Having noted the great success that EWS had with the introduction of the Class 66s at the end of the 1990s, Freightliner, which at the time was also using dated forms of traction for its operations, was inspired to press ahead and place an order. This was initially for five locos in 1998, but over the ensuing years, many more batches were ordered.

The standard locos, Class 66/5s, are basically identical to the EWS (now DB Cargo) fleet but were numbered in the 665xx range to differentiate the two companies. These are mostly used for intermodal trains and other light services. However, Freightliner soon decided that it needed a version that could handle heavier loads, such as coal and aggregates, so an order was placed for six Class 66/6 variants that have a lower top speed and modified gearing. Subsequently, 25 of these were produced, although six have since been exported to Poland.

Finally, Freightliner received seven low-emission Class 66/9s that are similar to the '66/5s' but with a lower fuel capacity so as to accommodate various other fittings. Despite being in service now for just over 20 years, the failure rate is very low, and I suspect we will be seeing them around for some years to come.

Chapter 1
Class 66/5

The Class 66/5 sub-class is exactly the same specification as the earlier EWS/DB examples but numbered in the 665xx series to reflect Freightliner ownership. They are regarded as standard locos and used for general duties as well as intermodal trains. They are occasionally used on some of the heavier trains run by the company, but usually only if a Class 66/6 is unavailable.

Right: The first of the Freightliner locos, 66501 *Japan 2001* is seen approaching Eastleigh with an unidentified Southampton Maritime-bound liner. 5 August 2004.

Below: Another of the early batch of locos, 66512 is seen approaching Eastleigh from the west with 6V36, the 10.38 Southampton Western Docks to Westbury, a train of imported stone. 25 March 2004.

This time we see 66505 passing through Swaythling, between Eastleigh and Southampton, with 4O14, the 07.00 Birch Coppice to Southampton Maritime. 13 November 2012.

Approaching Swaythling from the opposite direction is 66502 *Basford Hall Centenary 2001* with an unidentified northbound service from Southampton Maritime. 20 January 2005.

Threading its way through the city of Southampton, this is 66533 *Hanjin Express/Senator Express* with 4O49, the 09.23 Basford Hall to Southampton Maritime. This loco is unusual, as it carries two different names, one on each side. 10 August 2011.

Still looking quite new, 66565 is approaching Barnetby with an empty coal train headed for Immingham Docks. 7 March 2003.

Class 66/5/6/9

We are now in the London suburbs as 66520 passes Kensington Olympia with an unidentified westbound aggregates train. 29 October 2009.

Left: Looking in the opposite direction at Kensington Olympia a few months later, 66510 is leading a similar service, probably heading for Acton Yard. 18 March 2010.

Below: This time we are still in the London suburbs but a little further south as 66596 passes West Ealing with 6V04, the 08.02 Grain Oil Terminal to Colnbrook BAA Logistics loaded bogie tanks. This was a superb viewpoint before electrification. 28 January 2019.

Class 66/5

Southampton Maritime depot is the main stabling point/maintenance location in the south of England for Freightliner and carries out various forms of light repairs and exams on the locos. This is 66574 and 66501 *Japan 2001* on depot. 66574 has since been transferred to Colas Rail, renumbered and named as 66847 *Terry Baker*. 20 March 2009.

One of the main reasons behind the Class 66 design is for ease of maintenance, which is perfectly portrayed by this image of 66589 with a whole bodyside segment and roof section removed to access the engine at Maritime depot. 29 November 2013.

A few Christmas card scenes now! This is 66593 *3MG Mersey Multimodal Gateway* approaching Tilehurst after a significant snow fall (for this area at least) with 4O14, the 07.00 Birch Coppice to Southampton Maritime service. This loco carries specially designed non-standard nameplates. 22 December 2009.

On the same day as the previous shot, this is 66503 *The Railway Magazine* approaching Tilehurst from the east with 4M55, the 08.55 Southampton Maritime to Lawley Street service. This name was formerly carried by Class 43 HST power car 43197, which has since been scrapped. 22 December 2009.

A month later, and the snow had just started falling again, this time at Basingstoke as we see 66562 approaching on the Reading line with 4O14, the 07.00 Birch Coppice to Southampton Maritime service. 20 January 2010.

Right: From the same bridge but looking in the other direction with Basingstoke station in the background, this is 66542 heading north in something of a blizzard with 4M55, the 08.55 Southampton Maritime to Lawley Street. 20 January 2010.

Below: We are now further down the South West Main Line at Shawford as we see 66554 producing clouds of black exhaust heading north with 4M55, the 09.00 Southampton Maritime to Lawley Street. There was certainly something amiss with the loco's inner workings! 2 May 2019.

After some recent trackside clearance, this view just south of Shawford was opened up to allow this view of 66541 speeding south with 4O54, the 04.00 Leeds to Southampton Maritime service. Ten years on and this vegetation has all grown back even better than before. 21 December 2012.

During their career so far, not that many Freightliner locos have appeared on charter trains, This one was not actually planned and was a last minute stand in! The unusual combination of 66525 and 37059 is seen heading west near Dawlish at Coryton Cove with 1Z37, the 05.40 Worcester Shrub Hill to Penzance 'The Mazey Day Cornishman'. The train was due to have been hauled by 37069 and 37059, but 37069 failed before departure from Worcester with 37059 taking the train as far as Bristol Temple Meads, where 66525 was added; the South Devon banks would probably have been a bit too much for a solo Class 37 and ten coaches! 24 June 2017.

A very unusual place to see any sort of rail charter is in the freight yard at Westbury! This, however, is 66514 top and tailing 66105 with 1Z23, the 07.22 London Paddington to Bristol Temple Meads 'Only Freight Track and Horses' organised by Pathfinder Tours. The train visited various unusual lines in and around the Bristol area. It was also unusual in having both Freightliner and DB Cargo motive power. 11 September 2021.

An unusual place to see a Freightliner intermodal service this time, at least heading eastbound. This is 66539 with 4M58, the 10.27 Southampton Maritime to Basford Hall service, which for a short period in the early 2010s was routed via the South Western Main Line via Woking, and then the West Coast Main Line to Crewe. The train is seen at Totters Lane, between Hook and Winchfield. 2 September 2010.

During late 2010, the first few examples of Class 66/5 came off-lease with Freightliner and after a short time in store at Eastleigh were subsequently reused by other operators. This image depicts the first convoy with debranded 66579, 66578, 66580 and 66581 approaching Southampton Central running as 0Z90, the 14.13 Southampton Maritime to Eastleigh Works, to go into 'warm' storage. 22 October 2010.

Another off-lease convoy is seen passing Millbrook, this time 66575, 66576 and 66577 running as 0Z66, the 14.13 Southampton Maritime to Eastleigh Works. Interestingly, none of the locos have been debranded this time, with 66576 even still carrying its *Hamburg Sud Advantage* nameplates. Perhaps Freightliner was in a hurry to get rid of them or just didn't have time to remove things? 4 May 2011.

During the early days, Freightliner double-headers were quite unusual, but a triple-header was exceptional. This is 66559, 66557 and 66613 passing Millbrook with 6M16, the 13.48 Southampton Western Docks to Crewe Gresty Lane car train. I believe, on this occasion, the Class 66/6 had failed before departure, and for some reason two '66s' came to the rescue instead of one. Unfortunately, this popular train with photographers has long since been consigned to history. 14 January 2004.

Taken from a footbridge that has since been closed off due to 'safety issues', this is 66590 soon after departure with 4M61, the 12.55 Southampton Maritime to Trafford Park service. 20 March 2009.

Looking in the other direction from the same bridge, we see 66501 *Japan 2001* passing the terminal at Millbrook with 4051, the 09.36 Wentloog to Southampton Maritime, and approaching its destination. 20 March 2009.

Since the mid-2010s, all of the Class 66/5 locos have been in a common user pool, and former Heavy Haul sector examples can now be seen working intermodal trains and vice versa. This is illustrated here, as former intermodal dedicated 66501 *Japan 2001* is seen again, this time hauling an Acton to Theale stone train through Reading station. 15 October 2020.

Above: A mini loco profile now. During the mid-2000s, 66522 became something of a celebrity when half of the loco was painted lime green! It was repainted to acknowledge the partnership between Freightliner and the London waste firm of Shanks. The loco is seen to good effect stabled at Westbury station. 1 March 2005.

Right: Being a one-off livery, it was always going to be popular with photographers who all wanted to get the lime green end! 66522 and 66559 approach the junction with the South Western Main Line from Waterloo to Weymouth at Redbridge with a diverted 6O26, the 10.19 Hinksey Sidings to Eastleigh East Yard engineers' train. 31 December 2015.

The colourful pairing of 66522 and GBRf's 66721 *Harry Beck* is captured passing Basingstoke with 6Y48, the 09.00 Eastleigh Yard to Hoo Junction engineers' train. 28 September 2016.

After carrying its unique livery for 14 years, 66522 was finally returned to being 'just another Class 66' during September 2018 and is seen passing Salisbury with 7V07, the 11.47 Chichester to Westbury empty stone train. 20 July 2020.

Left: During a sudden downpour, this is 66501 *Japan 2001* coming off the line from Leamington Spa and Oxford at Coventry with an unidentified northbound intermodal service. 20 September 2007.

Below: Also on the West Coast Main Line, this is 66594 *NYK Spirit of Kyoto* heading south at Cow Roast (what a great name!), just south of Tring, with a service bound for Felixstowe. 4 March 2011.

In recent years, two Class 66/5s have been used as sort of mobile job advertisements for traincrew and ground staff. This is 66524 passing Stratford in East London with a northbound liner from Felixstowe. 29 April 2019.

Right: Taken from the viewing area of the well-known Sidings Hotel at Shipton-by-Beningbrough, just north of York, this is 66512 under a very moody sky heading north with a Heavy Haul coal train. 22 February 2008.

Below: A few images now depicting the sand train that used to run to/from Wool (Dorset) usually from Neasden, London, during the mid-2000s to mid-2010s. It was one of only a couple of regular freight trains in the county at the time, but there are even less as I write this! 66512 is seen again with the loaded train as it heads through Pokesdown, just east of Bournemouth, with 6M42, the 15.00 Wool to Neasden loaded train. 26 May 2006.

A couple of years later, and 66512 once again has charge of the train, this time seen near to Rockley Viaduct, just west of Hamworthy, as the 6O49 10.51 Neasden to Wool loaded service heads towards Holton Heath. This image was taken from a disused overbridge (since removed), which used to carry a single line from the nearby cordite factory that was built at Holton Heath in 1915. The complex had around 14 miles of its own narrow-gauge railways, including a line to a pier (long demolished) that was located behind the trees above the train from where cordite was dispatched by boat until 1938. 18 October 2008.

On a glorious late summer's day, this is 66530 heading south along the single line at West Stafford, between Moreton and Dorchester South, with the 6O49 empty train. As there are no loco run-round facilities in the sidings at Wool, as well as no direct access from the down main line, the train had to travel further west to Dorchester South to run-round. The train also had to split in half at Dorchester, with both parts then being tripped separately back up the ten miles or so to Wool. This loco was later exported and currently operates for Freightliner in Poland. 1 September 2010.

Another shot on the single line as 66566 approaches Dorchester South with the empty train. It is hard to believe now that this was a double track main line until 1985, when the seven miles or so between Moreton and Dorchester South was singled, supposedly for maintenance reasons. Ever since, there have been many occasions of late running brought about by this strange decision. 20 July 2006.

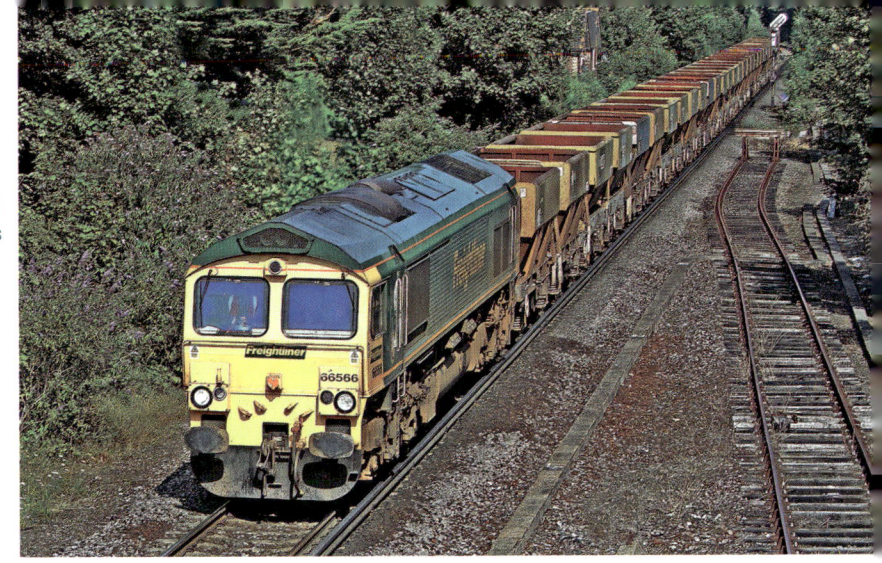

Right: Using just about all of its 3,300hp, this is a striking image of 66598 as it tops the rise about half a mile east of Wareham station with 6M42, the 15.00 Wool to Neasden loaded train. It could be heard for quite some time before actually coming into view. 11 November 2009.

Below: Part of the large expanse of Poole Harbour can be seen in this view of 66596 coming across Holes Bay causeway on a misty March afternoon with 6M42 as it approaches Poole. Many of the local railway workers of days gone by used to refer to this location as 'the mud'. 18 March 2009.

It is also interesting to note the various types of wagon used on this train; I believe these were not used for long due to difficulties with loading at Wool. 66549 is coming around the curve at Freemantle, just after passing through Southampton Central, with the 6O49 southbound empties. 15 March 2012.

The winter sun has almost set as 66595 is captured crossing the Redbridge causeway on the outskirts of Southampton with another loaded 6M42 on its way to London. 66595 was later exported to Poland. 2 February 2012.

Our final view of the Wool sand train for the time being shows 66531 with a brand-new rake of wagons passing Eastleigh East Yard heading south with the 6O49 empties. 17 April 2008.

There have been many instances of double-heading over the years, and a few examples of these are seen in this next batch of images. 66501 *Japan 2001* and 57005 *Freightliner Excellence* are approaching Eastleigh with an unidentified northbound liner from Southampton Maritime. The Class 57 was dispensed with by Freightliner back in 2008 and at the time of writing has been stored at West Coast Railways' depot at Carnforth since 2009. 24 January 2005.

Another '66/57' pairing as 66536 and 57003 *Freightliner Evolution* pass Millbrook with another unidentified service not far from its destination of Southampton Maritime. This Class 57 has fared slightly better, having been used by Direct Rail Services (DRS) from withdrawal by Freightliner in 2008, mainly on Railhead Treatment Trains (RHTT) and was finally stored in February 2022. More recently, though, it has been purchased by Locomotive Services. 16 January 2004.

As always with the railways of today, when we see a train with two or more locos on the front it usually means that either the original train loco has failed or there is a requirement for an extra loco at a certain location. There was never any need for two locos to power this train, especially as it was hardly loaded. 66519 and 66597 *Viridor* are approaching Eastleigh with 4O15, the 06.44 Lawley Street to Southampton Maritime. 14 January 2019.

With some fine autumn colours on show, 66518 and 66952 head south past Hinksey Yard, just south of Oxford, with 4O90, the 06.12 Leeds to Southampton Maritime service. 4 November 2011.

A little further south than the previous shot are 66537 and 66504, heading north at Didcot North Junction with a late-running 4M55, the 08.55 Southampton Maritime to Lawley Street service. The train loco here (which had possibly failed) was, at the time, the only example to wear the latest Powerhaul livery; but, as so often happens on the railway in the 21st century, things change rapidly, and this colour scheme has since been rendered obsolete in favour of Genesee & Wyoming orange and black. 20 January 2014.

A view now totally impossible due to the overhead catenary, 66588 and 66414 are passing Tilehurst with 4M55, the 08.55 Southampton Maritime to Ditton liner. 66414 has since received the now obsolete Powerhaul livery. 13 March 2014.

This time we see 66595 and 66415 approaching Eastleigh with 4M55, the 08,55 Southampton Maritime to Lawley Street liner. As mentioned earlier, 66595 is now working in Poland, but 66415 has received the latest Genesee & Wyoming orange and black livery and carries the name *You Are Not Alone*. 10 July 2017.

At the popular photographic spot of Worting Junction, just west of Basingstoke, we see 66596 and 66957 *Stephenson Locomotive Society 1909-2009* heading east with 4M55, the 08.55 Southampton Maritime to Lawley Street liner once again. These are two former Heavy Haul locos. 1 April 2019.

The Westbury area now sees plenty of Freightliner activity as a result of the company taking over the Mendip stone contract from DB Cargo in the late 2010s. 66540 *Ruby* and 66546 are passing Fairwood Junction and taking the station line, unusually double-heading 7A77, the 12.03 Merehead Quarry to Theale loaded train. 18 August 2020.

A pair of 'namers'! Well before electrification work started here, this is 66552 *Maltby Raider* and 66503 *The Railway Magazine* rapidly approaching Cholsey station on the Great Western Main Line. 66503 had failed before departure with 4L31, the 09.03 Bristol Freightliner Terminal to Felixstowe service, and required the assistance of then Freightliner Heavy Haul-allocated 66552 from nearby Stoke Gifford sidings. 12 October 2012.

At the time of this photograph, the area surrounding the western portal of Southampton Tunnel had just been cleared of the forest of trees that had grown up there over the years, affording this view of 66590 and 66567 passing through Central station with 4M61, the 12.55 Southampton Maritime to Trafford Park liner. Needless to say, during the ensuing 12 years, that forest of trees has grown back with a vengeance! 21 April 2010.

At the other end of Southampton Central, we see 66543 and 70017 passing through with 4O49, the 09.22 Crewe Basford Hall to Southampton Maritime service. This was a favoured spot of many steam photographers when trains could be seen beneath a magnificent semaphore signal gantry that used to stand where the colour light signal is now positioned, just below the clock tower on the right. 14 August 2012.

Above: One of just a few freight trains that currently use the Laverstock Junction (Salisbury) to Basingstoke section of line is 4M58, the 09.14 Southampton Maritime to Garston, which is seen passing Andover with 66548 and 70007 at the helm. 26 November 2018.

Left: This double-header was another one that occurred due to the train loco failing before departure. 66520 and 70001 *Powerhaul* are passing Salisbury station with 4O57, the 13.29 Wentloog to Southampton Maritime, which regularly runs via this route as opposed to the more usual one via Swindon and Basingstoke. 12 January 2022.

We now turn our attention to a few locos that have either changed their appearance over the years or have gone off to pastures new. This is 66573 departing Eastleigh after a crew change with a Southampton Maritime-bound liner. This loco is now perhaps better known as 66846 after being transferred to Colas Rail in the late 2000s. 31 October 2008.

Above: Next up we see 66574 approaching Southampton Central at Freemantle with 4M61, the 12.55 Southampton Maritime to Trafford Park liner. This loco was also later taken on by Colas Railfreight and renumbered/re-liveried as 66847 and carries the name *Terry Baker*. 11 February 2004.

Right: With part of the city of Bristol in the background, this is 66575 soon after passing through Temple Meads station with 4L32, the 11.00 Bristol Freightliner Terminal to Tilbury service. This loco is now 66848 and works for Colas Railfreight. 25 November 2010.

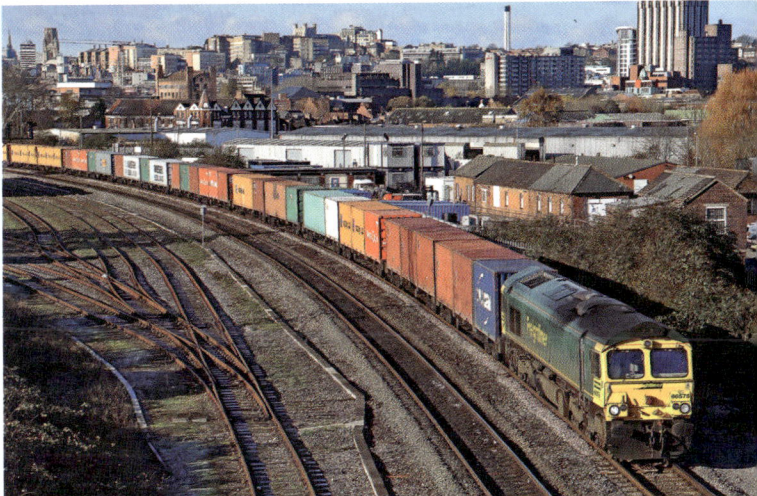

A fantastic view that has now been lost to electrification, this is 66577 passing South Moreton, just east of Didcot, with 4L32, the 11.00 Bristol Freightliner Terminal to Tilbury again. In a relatively short space of time, not only has the view been marred by the overhead catenary, but the imposing backdrop of the cooling towers at Didcot Power Station are no longer there, having been demolished in the mid-2010s. Even the loco itself has morphed into 66850 *David Maidment OBE* and is now operating for Colas Railfreight. 7 April 2011.

Class 66/5/6/9

Just about brand new and not even with any black deposits around the exhaust, this is an unusual perspective of 66578 earning its keep as the shunt loco at Millbrook terminal. This loco has since become 66738 *Huddersfield Town* and currently operates with GBRf. 15 April 2005.

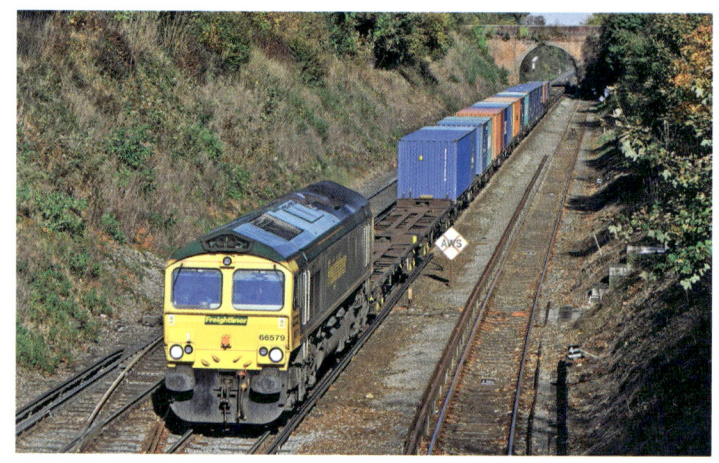

Left: This is 66579 powering south towards Winchester with an unidentified, but rather short, liner heading for Southampton Maritime. This loco also now plies its trade with GBRf under the guise of 66739 *The Bluebell Railway*. 31 October 2008.

Below: Next in line, and again almost brand new, this is 66580 approaching Eastleigh with an unidentified northbound liner from Southampton Maritime. This loco has now become 66740 *Sarah* and also operates for GBRf. 20 April 2005.

Class 66/5

The next couple of images depict locos that were not operational in the UK for that long before being exported to Poland during 2008/09. This is 66583 stabled in what was then the Freightliner sidings near the original Reading station, in fact the area where the loco is standing was later transformed into part of the new Reading Traincare Depot during the station rebuilding and redevelopment of the mid-2010s. 27 September 2007.

As all of the exported locos belonged to the Heavy Haul sector back then, not too many made their way very far west, as, at the time, there were very few Heavy Haul diagrams in the area. One, however, was the occasional trip from Fairwater Yard, near Taunton, to Westbury. Here we see 66584, which had just detached from this train at Westbury. It wasn't long after this that the loco was shipped to Poland. 28 March 2009.

Another mini loco profile now to show the changing appearance of 66504 in recent years. This is the loco in standard Freightliner livery crossing the River Thames over the Battersea Bridge at Chelsea with the southbound 4O86, the 05.03 Lawley Street to Thamesport liner. 17 September 2010.

Left: Three years later, the loco became the first of its class to be painted in the new Powerhaul livery. The immaculate ex-works machine is seen at Mount Pleasant level crossing, just south of St Denys, with 4O15, the 06.44 Lawley Street to Southampton Maritime service. 21 May 2013.

Below: A few months later, and a slightly dirtier 66504 is seen coming around the reverse curves at Sherrington in the Wylye Valley, just east of Warminster, with a diverted 4O51 09.36 Wentloog to Southampton Maritime service. 30 December 2013.

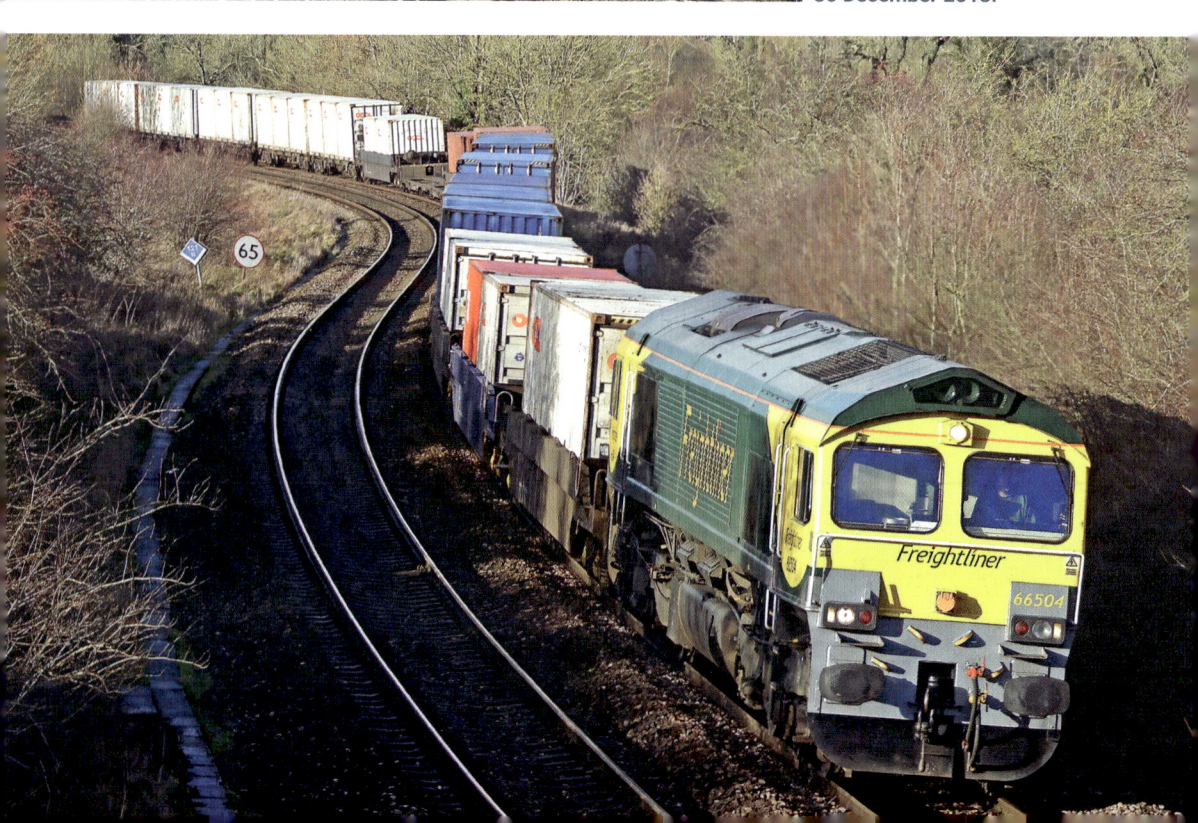

Not long after the previous picture was taken, it was decided that the grey front skirt/bufferbeam area didn't look quite right so it was repainted black, with all successive repaints into this livery being done in the same style. However, as mentioned earlier, this colour scheme was not destined to last. 66504 departs Eastleigh with 4O15, the 07.43 Hams Hall to Southampton Maritime. Note also that the fleet number on the front is painted green in this instance. 27 October 2014.

The next three images are of locos at work in Devon. This is 66548 passing the famous Langstone Rock and approaching Dawlish Warren with 6Y97, the 08.35 Aish Emergency Crossover to Westbury long-welded rail train. For the time of year, this was an unusually very windy day, as can be seen by the wet track and ballast, and spray whipping up in the background off the sea, which gave the loco's underframe a look of being new; it had just had a shower! 10 April 2016.

A few miles further east, and we see 66598 passing Powderham footbridge with another long-welded rail train as 6Y97, the 07.35 St. Erth to Westbury. The footbridge here replaced the dangerous foot crossing that can be seen beneath the loco. 1 September 2019.

Left: Here we see 66531 passing the delightful grade II-listed signal box at Crediton, which was built in 1875 and still very much open, with an Eggesford to Exeter Riverside empty ballast train. There was a major track renewal job going on in the vicinity at the time, which brought quite a few engineers' trains to this line. 15 October 2013.

Below: Back in Hampshire now, as 66595 passes through Southampton Central with 4M61, the 12.55 Southampton Maritime to Trafford Park service. Not long after the date of this image, the loco was exported to work in Poland. 29 February 2016.

The rare sight of a Freightliner coal train approaching Eastleigh! All is not what it seems, however. This is 66538 with 4O56, the 22.21 York Yard South to Eastleigh Works conveying wagons for scrapping. 18 October 2018.

The Wylye Valley line between Salisbury and Westbury is often used as a diversionary route when the more usual routes are closed for whatever reason, most often at weekends. This is 66541 passing the popular location of Little Langford, east of Warminster, with a diverted 4O22, the 01.47 Trafford Park to Southampton Maritime. 29 March 2013.

Exiting Fisherton Tunnel and passing Salisbury Tunnel Junction, this is 66501 *Japan 2001* taking the line to Romsey and Southampton with a diverted 4O15, the 07.43 Hams Hall to Southampton Maritime service. Just over six years later, on 31 October 2021, this was the scene of a very nasty crash involving a South Western Railway (SWR) Class 159/1 and a Great Western Railway Class 158, when the SWR unit could not stop on rails encrusted with crushed leaves, consequently colliding with the rear of the '158' at the tunnel mouth. Thankfully, there were no fatalities, but the SWR driver was trapped for some time before being released. 3 April 2015.

We now see 66541 approaching Colchester with a fully loaded train from Felixstowe. Many of the services originating at Felixstowe are shared between '66/5s' and Class 90s. 20 October 2011.

Intermodal services always look more impressive when they are loaded to capacity. This one certainly is, as 4M55, the 08.55 Southampton Maritime to Lawley Street, comes over the flyover at Worting Junction, just west of Basingstoke, with 66503 *The Railway Magazine* at the helm. 12 June 2014.

Seven years later, and the new look 66503 *The Railway Magazine* is seen passing Basingstoke with the same service, 4M55, the 08.55 Southampton Maritime to Lawley Street. This striking new livery was introduced in 2018 and has since been rather slowly applied to the Class 66s, with just a few examples so far painted in mid-2022. It is nice to see the nameplates are being kept in place upon repainting as well. 9 August 2021.

A bird's eye view of 66580 from a nearby multi-storey car park overlooking Eastleigh station as the loco brings 4O49, the 09.22 Crewe Basford Hall to Southampton Maritime, through platform two. This loco has since been taken on by GBRf under the guise of 66740 *Sarah*. 2 April 2009.

Some 19 years ago when this shot was taken, 66544 was still quite new, and this was a pretty rare sight of a Heavy Haul loco working an intermodal service, as locos in different pools tended to stick quite rigidly to their appropriate services back then. This particular service is 4O54, the 06.12 Leeds to Southampton Maritime. I suspect the original loco for this working failed before departure, and 66544 was the only replacement available. 27 August 2003.

On a fine autumnal afternoon, this is 66501 *Japan 2001* passing through St Denys with 4O49, the 09.22 Crewe Basford Hall to Southampton Maritime. The line to Portsmouth heads off behind the canopy to the right of the picture. 14 October 2011.

A few shots on the Basingstoke to Reading line now. A nice bright winter morning sees 66594 *NYK Spirit of Kyoto* shrouded in brake dust as it slows for the speed restriction on the reverse curves through Bramley, with 4M28, the 09.32 Southampton Maritime to Ditton. 2 February 2012.

More reverse curves, this time on the approach to Mortimer station, as 66564 heads south with 4O14, the 07.00 Birch Coppice to Southampton Maritime. I was glad this train was fully loaded, I don't think it would have worked quite so well otherwise. 19 August 2010.

Left: The bright yellow field is a giveaway as to the time of year! Fresh from a recent bogie overhaul, 66517 heads north through Mortimer with 4M55, the 08.55 Southampton Maritime to Lawley Street service. 28 April 2016.

Below: At the same location as the previous image, but showing a different perspective of the line taken from a public foot crossing, this is 66570 with 4M28, the 09.32 Southampton Maritime to Ditton. 22 August 2014.

Just west of Mortimer station, this time we see 66559 passing with 6X27, the 10.19 Hinksey Sidings to Eastleigh East Yard engineers' train. This train still runs today in the same timings (not usually as an X though) but is now operated by Colas Railfreight. 24 February 2016.

Right: Before the inevitable forest of trees and bushes shot up, this was the view from the entrance footpath to Micheldever station. 66590 comes around the curve with 4M28, the 09.32 Southampton Maritime to Ditton.
16 April 2013.

Below: The familiar location of Battledown Flyover, to the west of Basingstoke, this time as 66572 takes the Weymouth line with 4O51, the 09.58 Wentloog to Southampton Maritime service. The West of England line to Salisbury and Exeter passes beneath Battledown Flyover behind the loco.
13 September 2012.

Looking in the other direction at Battledown, this is 66556 about to pass over the flyover with 4M28, the 09.32 Southampton Maritime to Ditton. The concrete permanent way and fogman's huts used to be a common sight on the Southern Railway. 5 April 2016.

Left: Another well loaded train this time, as 66551 approaches Basingstoke with 4M55, the 08.32 Southampton Maritime to Lawley Street. 22 March 2022.

Below: Moving further west, with the city of Bristol dominating the view, this is 66531 passing Bristol Barton Hill depot with 6F90, the 10.50 Portbury to Fifoots Power Station (South Wales) coal train. This was a short-term flow that has long ceased to run. 20 January 2016.

6F90, the 10.50 Portbury to Fifoots Power Station coal train, is seen again as it breasts the climb out of the Severn Tunnel, with 66550 giving its all at the business end. The use of a 400mm lens here really emphasises the gradient. 17 February 2011.

Right: Moving north again to the first of a couple of shots at Leamington Spa as 66503 *The Railway Magazine* passes through with 4O49, the 09.23 Crewe Basford Hall to Southampton Maritime service. The wonderfully restored running in board can be seen to good effect. 24 September 2014.

Below: Looking in the other direction on the same day, we see 66587 passing through with 4M55, the 08.54 Southampton Maritime to Lawley Street service. There is always a superbly maintained floral display in the area to the right of the picture. 24 September 2014.

Class 66/5/6/9

Still at Leamington Spa, this is 66589 approaching from the Coventry direction with 4O54, the 06.12 Leeds to Southampton Maritime service. 24 September 2014.

Now for a few shots along the Great Western Main Line. Since the date this picture was taken, things have changed completely with the installation of overhead catenary. 66594 *NYK Spirit of Kyoto* approaches Swindon with 4L31, the 09.03 Bristol to Felixstowe service. 4 March 2014.

Class 66/5

Approaching Swindon from the east is the reasonably new 66596 with 4V60, the 10.57 Calvert to Bristol Barrow Road waste train. 3 December 2008.

A wonderful winter morning at Moulsford, just east of Cholsey, sees 66502 *Basford Hall Centenary 2001* passing with 4O14, the 07.00 Birch Coppice to Southampton Maritime. What a great shame it is to lose spots like this to the overhead electrification, but such is progress! 2 December 2011.

This time we see 66505 accelerating away from Didcot Parkway at South Moreton with 4O49, the 09.23 Crewe Basford Hall to Southampton Maritime service. 7 October 2011.

Above: Further east at the once very popular photographic location of Lower Basildon, this is 66536 heading towards Reading with 4O27, the 06.51 Ditton to Southampton Maritime. 28 October 2009.

Left: Dodging the shadows on a cold but lovely bright winter's day at Tilehurst is 66523, heading south with 4O15, the 06.44 Lawley Street to Southampton Maritime service. 7 January 2022.

Coming under the footbridge at Didcot North Junction is 66535 with 4M55, the 08.54 Southampton Maritime to Lawley Street service. This was one of the most recent locos sent to work in Poland during 2016. 30 June 2011.

This is 66559 passing through the wide cutting on the approach to Chippenham with 4V60, the 10.57 Calvert to Bristol Barrow Road waste train. Chippenham station, situated about a half a mile or so behind the camera, is the limit of electrification after the intended work to Bath and Bristol was cancelled due high costs. 13 July 2010.

66509 is seen approaching Stafford with a rake of empty coal hoppers from Rugeley Power Station. 23 January 2009.

This is an immaculate 66576 *Hamburg Sud Advantage* coming to a stop at Eastleigh station for a crew change with 4M55, the 08.54 Southampton Maritime to Lawley Street. At this time, the loco was only four months old and had been named just a few days prior to this shot. It remained in this guise until mid-2011, when it was transferred to Colas Railfreight. Now carrying the latter's house colours, it is renumbered as 66849 and also named *Wylam Dilly*. 2 July 2004.

At the same spot as the previous image, but almost 17 years later, this is 66511 with the same 4M55, the 08.54 Southampton Maritime to Lawley Street service. Note also the veteran Class 20s to the left of the picture waiting to proceed onto the works to collect some coaching stock. 13 April 2021.

Showing signs of a recent bogie overhaul, 66516 is just about to pass beneath Freemantle footbridge, on the approach to Southampton Central, with 4M61, the 12.55 Southampton Maritime to Trafford Park service. 5 June 2013.

Another load of brand-new cars is slowly brought out of the docks complex at Southampton as 66527 *Don Raider* approaches Millbrook station with 6M16, the 13.48 Southampton Western Docks to Crewe Gresty Lane. This is another of the recent exports to Poland during 2016. 23 July 2004.

A late autumn afternoon with the sun getting low, 66502 *Basford Hall Centenary 2001* is approaching Mount Pleasant level crossing with 4O54, the 06.15 Leeds to Southampton Maritime service. 22 November 2013.

The well-known vantage point of Campbell Road bridge at Eastleigh this time as we see 66529 departing with 4O15, the 06.44 Lawley Street to Southampton Maritime service. This is one of the fleet that has recently undergone cab refurbishments, including new light clusters. 24 September 2021.

The first of three images that show the livery change recently applied to 66587. In standard Freightliner livery, here is the loco approaching Oxford with a lengthy 4O15, the 07.43 Hams Hall to Southampton Maritime service. 13 November 2013.

Six years later, and the loco now looks like this! 66587 *As One We Can* is approaching Basingstoke soon after its striking repaint into pink and white livery with 4M55, the 09.00 Southampton Maritime to Lawley Street service. This is essentially the new Genesee & Wyoming livery but with the orange replaced by pink and the black replaced by white. Certainly no mistaking this one! 11 June 2019.

Above: Another shot of this unmistakeable loco as it departs from Eastleigh with a very lightly loaded 4O18, the 07.24 Lawley Street to Southampton Maritime service. 11 August 2020.

Left: The line between Redbridge and Romsey is often utilised as a diversionary route, mostly at weekends, but there are a couple of Freightliner services booked via the line during weekdays. This is 66597 *Viridor* approaching Mottisfont & Dunbridge with 4M67, the 14.17 Southampton Maritime to Hams Hall, which is booked via Romsey and Andover to Basingstoke. 7 February 2019.

Not exactly an everyday sight at Gillingham (Dorset), where any sort of loco is rare. This is 66563 passing through with 0Z66, the 08.30 Southampton Maritime to Exeter St Davids route learning run. Although the signal box behind the loco looks relatively modern, it was closed back in 2011 when the line was re-signalled and is now kept in situ purely as a ground frame to work the siding points seen in the foreground. 20 July 2022.

At the time, this was believed to be the first appearance of a Freightliner Class 66/5 further south than Poole. Engineering work and track relaying was taking place west of Hamworthy and 66535, temporarily hired in by EWS, is seen awaiting its next move at the station. Once again, the signal box in the background was taken out of use during 2011 but this time demolished soon after. The loco itself has subsequently been exported to Poland. 12 November 2005.

Right: The next station south of Hamworthy is Holton Heath, where we see 66522 approaching along the lengthy gun barrel straight stretch of line from Wareham, around two miles distant, with an engineers' train from a relaying site near Dorchester returning to Eastleigh Yard. 25 October 2020.

Below: On the same day as the previous shot, 66592 *Johnson Stevens Agencies* is captured passing Holton Heath station with another engineers' train returning to Eastleigh Yard from the same relaying site. The name carried by this loco was first carried by 37154, until it was withdrawn and scrapped. 25 October 2020.

To end this section on the Class 66/5s, we see some shots taken around the Castle Cary/Westbury area, which has become a good place to see Freightliner activity in recent years. This is 66524 passing Castle Cary station with a late-running 6M40 10.32 Exeter Riverside to Cliffe Hill Stud Farm, which only ran for a short time. It has since been re-timed to start from Westbury using Colas traction. 9 January 2014.

Taken with the aid of a drone, this is 66560 passing Wyke Champflower, just east of Castle Cary, with a huge 6X37, the 09.35 Didcot North Junction to Fairwater Yard (Taunton) high output ballast cleaner (HOBC) train. 10 April 2022.

Around half a mile east of the previous image, and passing between a couple of nice patches of Rosebay Willowherb, this is 66562 at Cole, just south of Bruton, with 6Y40, the 08.20 Newton Abbot to Westbury engineers' train. 66618 *Railways Illustrated Photographic Awards* was bringing up the rear. 14 July 2019.

This time we see 66561 running late with a rather short 6C72, the 08.40 Fairwater Yard to Westbury approaching Bruton station. Strangely, the building behind the loco is nothing to do with the railway and never has been. It was built in quite recent times and is actually a car maintenance garage. The builder obviously has railway interests! 21 July 2021.

Further east along the line, we reach Frome and the nearby Berkeley Marsh, where we see 66540 *Ruby* heading east with a late running 6M20, the 10.38 Whatley Quarry to Churchyard Sidings (St Pancras) stone train. 22 July 2020.

We have now reached the outskirts of Westbury as 66565 is seen passing Masters Crossing, just west of Fairwood Junction, with a late running 7A77, the 11.48 Merehead Quarry to Theale loaded stone train. 26 August 2020.

The crossing seen in the previous image is just beyond the rear of the train in this shot as 66528 *Madge Elliot MBE - Borders Railway Opening 2015* is seen passing Fairwood Junction and taking the line via Westbury station with 6A60, the 08.32 Whatley Quarry to Oxford Banbury Road stone train. The Powerhaul livery applied to this loco and a couple of others has since been superseded by Genesee & Wyoming orange and black.
3 September 2021.

Approaching the next bridge, a little further east from Fairwood Junction seen in the previous image, this is 66514 nearing Lambert's Bridge with 6M20, the 10.38 Whatley Quarry to Churchyard Sidings (St Pancras) stone train.
25 November 2021.

The bridge that the previous image was taken from can be seen in this view of 66526 *Driver Steve Dunn (George)* and its short train almost merging in with the surrounding countryside as it passes with 6C84, the 08.40 Fairwater Yard to Westbury. 26 April 2018.

A very dark sky looks threatening in the background as 66531 approaches Westbury with 6F21, the 05.36 North Somerset Junction (Bristol) to Westbury engineers' train, running some 535 minutes late! 1 November 2018.

Looking somewhat lonely, this is 66506 *Crewe Regeneration* going away from the camera and approaching Heywood Junction, near Westbury, with an unknown light engine move heading east up the Berks & Hants line towards Newbury. 13 January 2012.

With the lines to/from the Berks & Hants main line leading off to the left, this is 66597 *Viridor* passing Hawkeridge Junction with the occasional 4V54, the 10.14 Southampton Maritime to Avonmouth West Wharf. I happened to be in the right place at the right time, as very often this runs almost at the drop of a hat! 22 May 2018.

This time we see 66520 leaning into the curve soon after passing Avoncliffe with 6C73, the 12.22 Westbury Yard to Fairwater Yard via Bristol. This train usually runs via the direct route from Westbury to Taunton via Somerton, but occasionally it runs via Bath and Bristol to get the train the right way round for operating its next service. 20 January 2017.

The last shot in this section sees 66547 just a short distance from the previous image with 6M36, the 12.00 Westbury Lafarge to Earles Sidings cement train, which was another rather erratic runner, and sometimes still is. 30 March 2012.

Chapter 2
Class 66/6

There were originally 25 of this sub-class, with six examples having now been exported to Poland. All are specially geared for hauling some of the company's heavier oil and stone trains. They also have a lower maximum top speed of 65mph, as opposed to 75mph for a '66/5' or '66/9'.

This is first of the sub-class, 66601 *The Hope Valley*, creeping along the down loop line just west of Southampton Central with 6M16, the 13.48 Southampton Western Docks to Crewe Gresty Lane car train. 5 March 2004.

A very new 66616 is captured heading north through St Denys with the same train as the previous image, the 6M16 13.48 Southampton Western Docks to Crewe Gresty Lane. The two wagons behind the loco, I believe, were some sort of trial to offer the vehicles in transit further protection, but they never seemed to be used a great deal on this service. In any case, Freightliner ceased operating this train during the mid-2000s. 26 March 2004.

This time we see 66611 in the loading bay for the new vehicles adjacent to Millbrook station. The train often split into two parts to load but reformed when the loading was completed before departure. This loco has since been exported to work for Freightliner in Poland. 6 October 2005.

In the early 2000s, when Railways Illustrated magazine used to run an annual photographic competition, 66618 was named *Railways Illustrated Annual Photographic Awards* with an additional small plate added below to signify the photographer that won in each particular year. Unfortunately, after only about two years, the competition was abolished, but the loco still carries the name to this day and the last winner. It is seen here taking the docks line with 6O36, the 07.45 Eastleigh Yard to Southampton Western Docks, which was later loaded with stone and tripped to Westbury. 1 September 2004.

Some 15 years later, 66618 *Railways Illustrated Annual Photographic Awards* is seen passing Salisbury with 6V62, the 13.21 Southampton Up Yard to Whatley Quarry empty stone train. Note the new headlight clusters on the front and also what appears to be a bit of a dent along the side panel. 1 April 2019.

Another Christmas card scene as 66606 heads south through Oxford with an exceptionally late 6V14 22.38 Cliffe Hill Stud Farm to Westbury loaded ballast train, the train presumably having been massively delayed by the weather conditions. This is still a runner today but now employing Colas traction. 7 January 2010.

Class 66/5/6/9

Here we see 66604 heading through platform two at Eastleigh and passing beneath the rather ornate footbridge with 6V16, the 11.55 Fareham to Whatley Quarry empty stone train. 21 January 2022.

6V16, the 11.55 Fareham to Whatley Quarry, is seen again, this time passing beneath the distinctive stone conveyor at Botley terminal with 66617 at the helm. Botley still sees a regular delivery of stone by rail from the Mendip quarries but usually during the hours of darkness. 14 July 2021.

Class 66/6

A profile of the still relatively new 66620 awaiting its next move in the sidings next to Westbury station. Note the small unofficial stickered name *Buccaneer* above the radiator grilles! 30 August 2006.

A few more images of the sand train that used to run to Wool, Dorset, for which a '66/6' was more suited due to the formidable steep bank it had to tackle between Poole and Branksome with a heavy load on its return. This is 66602 passing what would become the last manually worked gated crossing on the Waterloo to Weymouth line at East Stoke, about two miles east of Wool, with 6M42, the 15.00 Wool to Neasden loaded train. 14 January 2008.

This time we see 66608 heading south through the New Forest National Park at Lymington Junction, about a mile or so from Brockenhurst, with 6O49, the 10.51 Neasden to Wool empties. The branch line to Lymington can be glimpsed to the right of the picture. This loco was later exported and now operates in Poland. 2 March 2010.

Left: This is an earlier shot of the train during the time four-wheel hopper wagons were used, as 66604 is seen approaching Poole in the setting sun with the 6M42 loaded northbound service. 29 November 2006.

Below: The uniformity of the train is interrupted by just one white wagon as 66613 rolls across the causeway at Holes Bay on the approach to Poole with 6M42. 17 September 2008.

With the driver ready to check that his train has cleared the siding, this is 66622 pulling away from Wool with 6M42, again during the period that four-wheel hoppers were used. The loco was still quite new at this time. 6 December 2006.

Right: This is 66615 with an empty train passing a foot crossing at East Burton, just west of Wool, as it heads for Dorchester South with 6O49, where it will split and run-round back to Wool. 8 September 2010.

Below: Another pretty reliable Class 66/6 turn is the cement trains that run to/from Theale in Berkshire. This is 66610 heading east through Reading station with 6M91, the 13.10 Theale to Hope (Earles Sidings). 7 April 2021.

Class 66/5/6/9

This is a vantage point that was only obtainable for a short time while the reconstruction of Reading station was taking place and before the overhead wires were erected. This is 66605 coming off the West of England line from Newbury and negotiating its way through Reading station with 6M91, the 11.13 Theale to Earles Sidings cement train. This is another loco that had recently undergone cab refurbishment. 14 January 2015.

6M91, the 11.13 Theale to Earles Sidings cement train, is seen again, this time with 66614 *Poppy 1916-2016* powering through Twyford on the Great Western Main Line. 1 September 2017.

Class 66/6

About a mile or so east of the previous shot, this is 66616 passing Ruscombe with 6M91 11.13 Theale to Earles Sidings again. Needless to say, this fine view is now lost to electrification. 1 October 2015.

Very occasionally. it was possible to capture 6V94, the 07.35 Earles Sidings to Theale train, but it was very rare. However, I got lucky on this day, as 66619 *Derek W. Johnson MBE* is seen approaching Twyford. 17 September 2014.

Another rare sight is a '66/6' working an intermodal train as their lower top speed and modified gearing is not really suited to this type of train. This, however, is 66607 passing Lower Basildon on the Great Western Main Line with 4M61, the 12.54 Southampton Maritime to Trafford Park service. It was thought that the rostered loco failed before departure, and this loco was the only spare one in the area at the time. 28 October 2009.

Left: This is 66603 passing through Parson Street, on the outskirts of Bristol. with a Fairwater Yard (Taunton) to Westbury HOBC working. The more usual route for these trains is direct via Castle Cary, but occasionally the whole train needs to be turned, hence going the long way round. 11 March 2011.

Below: The bridge the previous shot was taken from can be seen in the distance as 66610 heads through Parson Street towards Bristol with a similar working. 27 August 2010.

Moving further east, we see 66607 approaching Swindon on a very cold winter's afternoon with an unidentified westbound stone working.
3 December 2008.

All the wonderful infrastructure in the image has since been consigned to the history books, unfortunately. The almost new 66605 contrasts with the old wooden signal box and semaphore signals as it heads through Barnetby with an oil train from Immingham.
7 March 2003.

A nice uniform rake of hopper wagons this time as we see 66603 approaching North Staffordshire Junction, south of Derby, with the 4E42 10.00 Rugeley Power Station to Barnetby Down Reception Sidings. 11 February 2016.

This is 66612 *Forth Raider* with a huge HOBC train heading north past Brent Knoll on the Taunton to Bristol route. 66616 was bringing up the rear of the train, which was almost half a mile long! 66612 has since been exported and is now working in Poland. 5 June 2010.

Back on the Great Western Main Line, this is 66621 approaching Foxhall Junction, just west of Didcot Parkway, with 6M40, the 11.55 Westbury to Cliffe Hill Stud Farm empty ballast boxes. This train still runs today but is now worked by Colas traction. 8 October 2009.

66623 is unique amongst all sub-classes of Freightliner '66s' as it has never carried the standard green livery applied to all other locos from new. It was delivered in a rather nice shade of blue with Bardon Aggregates decals on the bodysides. The immaculate loco, just seven months old, is seen at Rugby. 20 September 2007.

Right: By the time of this photo, 66623 had received its *Bill Bolsover* nameplates and is seen near Winfrith, just west of Wool, with 6O49, the 10.51 Neasden to Wool empty sand train. 7 September 2013.

Below: Unusually running on a Saturday, and even more unusually not starting from Neasden, this is 66623 *Bill Bolsover* again, this time passing Bapton in the Wylye Valley, between Warminster and Salisbury, with 6O49, the 12.40 Theale to Wool empty sand train. 11 January 2014.

Our final view of 66623 *Bill Bolsover* in blue livery sees it approaching Dorchester South with the 6O49 from Neasden, where it will divide and run in two parts up to Wool. 25 May 2010.

During 2019, the loco was repainted in what is currently the latest Genesee & Wyoming Freightliner livery of orange and black, the loco also lost its name some years prior to this. Here it is departing Eastleigh with 6V62, the 13.21 Southampton Up Yard to Whatley Quarry empty stone train. 6 May 2021.

This is a curious train than ran for a couple of years in the mid-2000s. Approaching Eastleigh is a practically new 66606 with 6V36, the 10.38 Southampton Western Docks to Westbury loaded train of imported stone, which was unloaded at Westbury virtual quarry. It was a bit strange as the two huge stone quarries of Whatley and Merehead are only a few miles from Westbury! 27 August 2003.

A fine early autumn morning at a foot crossing near Witham Friary, west of Westbury, sees 66622 passing with 6C72, the 08.20 Fairwater Yard to Westbury train consisting of part of a HOBC. 25 September 2012.

With dust from a loaded stone train just disappearing into the distance blowing across the fields, 66603 heads west at Berkeley Marsh, near Frome, with 6C58, the 12.10 Oxford Banbury Road to Whatley Quarry empties. 22 July 2020.

Coming up the long straight on the approach to Fairwood Junction, Westbury, this is 66605 with 6M20, the 10.38 Whatley Quarry to Churchyard Sidings (St Pancras) loaded stone train. This loco was involved in a bit of an altercation during 2021 but has since returned to traffic in 2022, having been repaired and repainted in Genesee & Wyoming orange and black Freightliner livery. 18 August 2020.

Left: Soon after leaving its point of origin and with the famous white horse on the hillside as a giveaway, 66609 is approaching Lambert's Bridge with 6C73, the 12.12 Westbury to Fairwater Yard consisting of a part HOBC train. This is another loco that has since been sent to work for Freightliner in Poland. 9 December 2010.

Below: At the same spot 11 years later, 66621 is heading west with 6C68, the 11.38 Avonmouth to Whatley Quarry empties as 7A77, the 12.03 Merehead to Theale, passes in the opposite direction. 30 March 2021.

Above: Coasting through Castle Cary is 66607 with the 6C84 13.19 Westbury Yard to Fairwater Yard. It looks as if I am close to the track here, but I was actually safely standing right on the very end of the down platform. 9 January 2014.

Right: 66618 *Railways Illustrated Annual Photographic Awards* is seen passing Heywood Village, just north of Westbury on the Trowbridge line, with 7B12, the 11.23 Merehead Quarry to Wootton Basset loaded stone train. 5 April 2022.

Back at Fairwood Junction, this is 66601 *The Hope Valley* passing with 6C68, the 11.38 Avonmouth to Whatley Quarry empties. 3 September 2021.

This time 66622 is passing Fairwood Junction with a very late running 6M20, the 10.38 Whatley Quarry to Churchyard Sidings (St Pancras) loaded stone train. 3 September 2021.

For a while, Freightliner had an operating base in the old sidings that now form part of the new Reading Traincare Depot, with locos regularly stabling there between duties. One of the more elusive of the sub-class was 66624, which was exported to Poland quite soon after it entered service in the UK. 11 September 2008.

Passing through Salisbury in the early autumn sunshine, 66617 has charge of 6V62, the 13.21 Southampton Up Yard to Whatley Quarry empty stone train. 29 September 2021.

66608 is seen curving round off the line from East Croydon with an unidentified train about to head through Clapham Junction. This loco is now working for Freightliner in Poland. 12 August 2010.

66618 *Railways Illustrated Annual Photographic Awards* is passing through Severn Tunnel Junction station with 6Z50, the 11.23 Pengam to Wool empty sand train. I am not entirely sure how the wagons ended up in South Wales but this working was a one off. 30 September 2014.

To conclude this section on the Class 66/6s, this is 66622 again on the approach to Oxford station with 6A60, the 08.32 Whatley Quarry to Oxford Banbury Road stone train. 16 February 2022.

Chapter 3
Class 66/9

This small sub-class of just seven locos were designed as a lower emission version, and as a result have a smaller fuel capacity so as to accommodate various other components that had to be added to the design. In all other respects, they are similar to Class 66/5s and can be seen hauling any of the company's trains throughout the UK.

Left: About to pass through Castle Cary station is 66951 with 6C73, the 12.12 Westbury to Fairwater Yard (Taunton) engineers' train. 16 July 2015.

Below: 66951 is seen again, this time rounding the curve between Kew New Junction and Kew East Junction with 6M79, the 10.56 Angerstein Wharf to Bardon Hill empty stone train. 30 April 2010.

Above: Setting off from a short signal check at Derby station is 66953 with an unidentified southbound coal train.
5 March 2009.

Right: The first of a few shots showing double-headers sees 66951 and 66505 approaching Basingstoke with 4M58, the 09.32 Southampton Maritime to Garston service. 11 May 2017.

Now completely transformed by electrification, 66935 and 66558 are approaching Didcot Parkway with 4L31, the 09.03 Bristol to Felixstowe North service.
28 September 2015.

There is still a fine view to be had above the twin tunnels at Popham, near Micheldever, as we see 66954 and 66416 powering by with 4M55, the 08.53 Southampton Maritime to Lawley Street. The '66/9' became one of the most recent examples exported to Poland during 2016, and the '66/4' received the now obsolete Powerhaul livery soon after this photograph was taken. 16 July 2014.

Taken from the former footbridge at Millbrook station, 66952 and 70007 pass through as they near their destination with 4O90, the 06.12 Leeds to Southampton Maritime. The footbridge here was removed (or at least truncated) during 2020. 23 April 2018.

The final loco delivered to Freightliner, and the highest numbered Class 66 in the UK, this is 66957 *Stephenson Locomotive Society 1909-2009* approaching West Drayton with an unidentified westbound train of empty box wagons. 31 August 2012.

66957 *Stephenson Locomotive Society 1909-2009* is seen again as it approaches Hawkeridge Junction with 6Y66, the 10.00 Cardiff East to Westbury engineers' train. 21 November 2015.

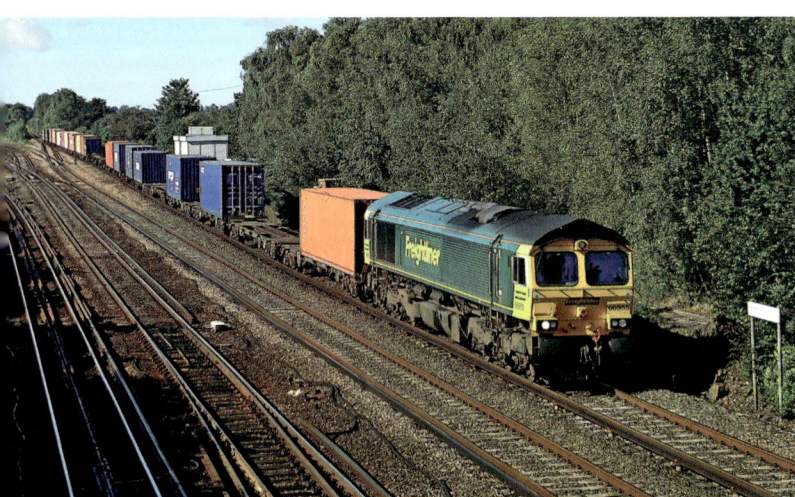

Above: Soon after passing through Bath Spa, 66951 is now approaching Oldfield Park with 4V31, the 07.53 London Gateway to Bristol, a service that no longer runs. 17 July 2018.

Left: With Battledown Flyover visible in the distance, this is 66955 passing Worting Junction with a late running 4M55, the 08.55 Millbrook to Lawley Street. 13 September 2012.

Another view of 66955 but this time powering south on the approach to Didcot North Junction with 4O14, the 07.43 Hams Hall to Southampton Maritime service. Originally, the electrification was due to obliterate this view, but spiralling costs saw the scheme to Oxford being curtailed. 1 October 2014.

A few more shots of the Wool sand train now, which, although usually used by a '66/6', also saw the other two sub-classes sometimes substituted. Pulling away from the point of origin, this is 66957 *Stephenson Locomotive Society 1909-2009* with 6M42, the 15.00 Wool Sidings to Neasden. This train no longer runs – there have been rumblings for many years now that GBRf would be taking it on, but to date this has come to nothing. 22 April 2010.

A month earlier, and in dire weather conditions, the same locomotive as in the previous image has charge of the same train as it battles the 1 in 60/1 in 50 gradient through Parkstone station. The train was quite literally down to walking pace at this point with the heavy load and doing very well on the damp rails. 23 March 2010.

Above: Far better weather conditions this time as 66953 drifts past West Stafford, just east of Dorchester, with 6O49, the 10.51 Neasden to Wool empties. As can be seen from the space for an extra track to the right, this was once a double track main line, but a curious decision was made to single this section between Moreton and Dorchester South as mentioned earlier in this volume. 9 July 2009.

Left: A couple of years later, and 66953 has charge of 6O49 once again and is seen this time powering down the long straight section of track between Holton Heath and Wareham at Keysworth Crossing. 3 September 2011.

At a tricky location to get to in the heart of the New Forest National Park, this is 66957 *Stephenson Locomotive Society 1909-2009* at Deerleap foot crossing, about a mile or so south of Ashurst station, with 6O49. About the only way to get here is a walk via a long forest track, but it was worth it in the end! 21 April 2010.

Above: Further west now as we see 66951 forging along near the former Charlton Mackrell station with the heavy 6X08, the 08.10 Ruscombe (near Twyford) to Fairwater Yard (Taunton) engineers' train, 66561 was bringing up the rear.
13 June 2021.

Right: Unfortunately, the stand of Rosebay Willowherb prominent in the foreground is now past its best, but 66953 is certainly not as it heads west along the Frome avoiding line with 6C73, the 12.12 Westbury to Fairwater Yard with a HOBC portion.
12 August 2020.

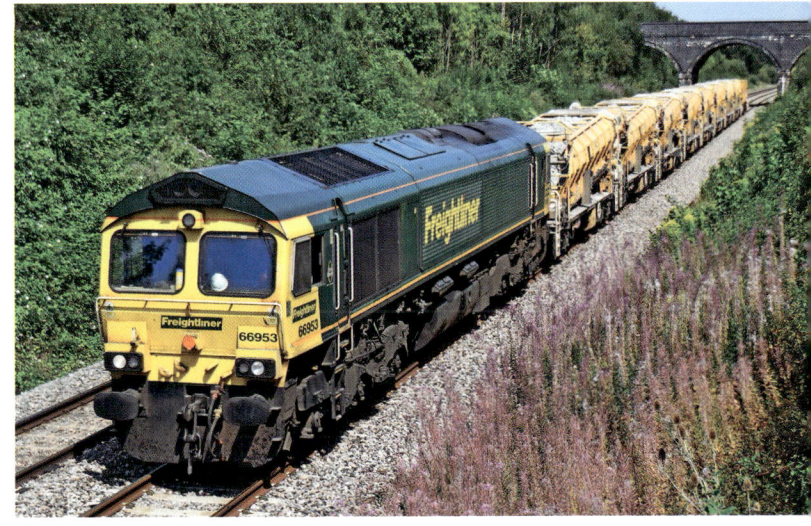

Glimpsed through a convenient hole in the hedge, this is 66953 passing Berkeley Marsh, between Westbury and Frome, with 6Y15, the 08.27 Oxford to Fairwater Yard HOBC train. 66415 was on the rear but well out of site in this shot.
13 September 2020.

Above: Pulling along by the station at Westbury is 66952 with 6A60, the 08.32 Whatley Quarry to Oxford Banbury Road loaded stone train. The platform has recently been extended here, affording a good view of the yard. 25 November 2021.

Left: Part of the distinctive city of Bath is the backdrop as 66956 approaches Bath Spa station with 4V31, the 07.53 London Gateway to Bristol. 5 September 2018.

This time the various buildings forming the city of Bristol are dominating the background as 66952 slowly passes through Temple Meads station and on to the Bath and Chippenham line with 4L32, the 11.00 Bristol to Tilbury. This image was taken from the St Philip's Causeway road bridge. 13 January 2012.

Above: This is 66955 during shunting operations at Bristol Freightliner Terminal. Although this terminal is no longer used for container traffic, it does occasionally see stone trains, usually worked by a DCR Class 60. 17 March 2015.

Right: 66954 is captured at Norton Bavant, just east of Warminster, with a diverted 4O51, the 09.58 Wentloog to Southampton Maritime service. A blockade was in place around the Reading area at this time. 29 March 2013.

A few years prior to this x, when 66957 *Stephenson Locomotive Society 1909-2009* was a Heavy Haul dedicated loco, sights such as this on an intermodal service would have been quite rare. The loco passes through Basingstoke with 4O90, the 06.12 Leeds to Southampton Maritime service. 10 November 2017.

A very clean 66954 is seen approaching Basingstoke with 4M55, the 08.53 Southampton Maritime to Lawley Street. This loco is currently working in Poland. 8 June 2015.

Left: 66955 is negotiating the crossings at the east end of Basingstoke station as it comes off the line from Reading with 4O90, the 06.12 Leeds to Southampton Maritime. 5 January 2016.

Below: Heading south past Worting Junction is 66954 with 4O14, the 05.36 Garston to Southampton Maritime service. It was soon after this date that the loco was exported to work in Poland. 20 September 2017.

An almost-new 66956 is powering north at Shawford with a largely empty 4E44, the 09.36 Millbrook to Leeds, a service that has long since ceased to run. 29 May 2009.

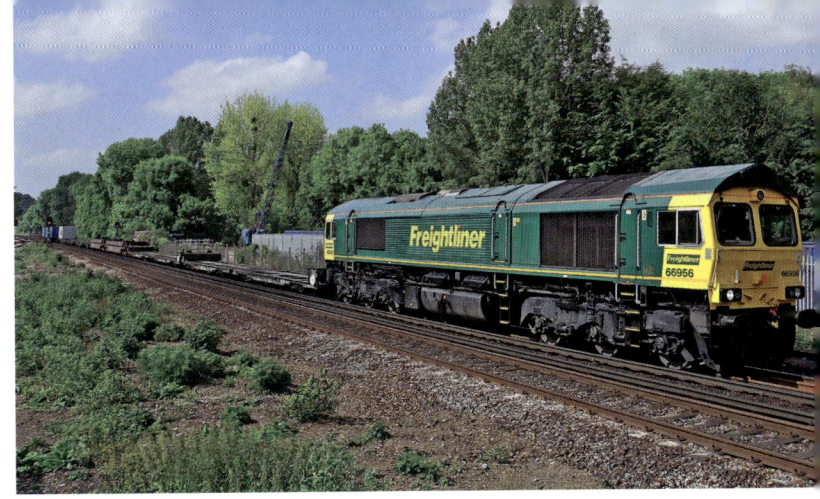

Right: Some 13 years later, and 66951 is passing the same spot as in the previous picture with 4M55, the 08.32 Southampton Maritime to Lawley Street. 30 March 2022.

Below: This is 66952 engaged in shunting in the yard at Eastleigh. 2 January 2014.

Above: The steep rise out of the Severn Tunnel is seen to good effect as 66953 heaves 6M04, the 11.50 Portbury to Rugeley Power Station, over the summit and approaches the station at Severn Tunnel Junction. This view is now of course impossible with the advent of electrification. 30 September 2014.

Left: Still in South Wales, 66955 is crossing the River Usk at Newport with 4O51, the 09.58 Wentloog to Southampton Maritime. The ruins of Newport Castle can be seen on the left. 19 April 2013.

Passing a public foot crossing just north of Mortimer, on the Basingstoke to Reading line, 66954 has charge of 4M58, the 09.32 Southampton Maritime to Ditton service. 12 May 2015.

Above: The aforementioned foot crossing from which the previous image was taken is just out of site at top left of this view as 66952 heads south with 6X26, the 10.19 Hinksey Sidings to Eastleigh East Yard conveying side-loading point carrier wagons. This train (usually running as 6O26) is now in the hands of Colas Railfreight. 13 January 2016.

Right: A few shots on the Great Western Main Line now. An observer at this spot today would be hard pushed to figure out that it is the same place. The footbridge in the background has been replaced by a horrible new caged structure and masts, and wires litter the whole scene. 66954 is approaching Tilehurst with 4O54, the 06.13 Leeds to Southampton Maritime. 26 May 2011.

66955 comes round the curve just west of Pangbourne with 4M55, the 08.55 Southampton Maritime to Lawley Street service. Despite the overhead masts, I believe this shot might still be possible in 2022? 21 October 2009.

Above: The remains of the once-famous GWR loco works at Swindon can be seen behind the train as 66956 approaches Swindon station with 4L31, the 09.03 Bristol to Felixstowe service. 28 October 2014.

Left: Such are the timings of some of these Freightliner services, especially on the Great Western Main Line, that I was able to get a train from Swindon and get another shot of 66956 on the same train as in the previous shot! It is seen waiting to proceed towards Didcot Parkway station. 28 October 2014.

Approaching Mount Pleasant level crossing, just south of St Denys, this is 66954 with a very well loaded 4O54, the 06.15 Leeds to Southampton Maritime. 7 May 2014.

Apart from a regular stone train from the Somerset quarries to Woking that has been Freightliner operated since 2019, prior to this Freightliner locos were never that common east of Basingstoke on the South Western Main Line. This is 66957 approaching Farnborough with a diverted 6Z26, the 05.09 Bescot to Eastleigh East Yard engineers' train. The usual arrangement for the running of this train is 6V25 Bescot to Hinksey Sidings (Oxford) and then forwards a little later as 6O26 to Eastleigh East Yard. 12 August 2016.

66956 at the delightfully named location of Cow Roast, just south of Tring, is powering by with an unidentified service, probably heading for Felixstowe. 4 March 2011.

To end this volume on the Freightliner Class 66s, we see the newest loco of the fleet for the last time, but in a spot far from where it might be expected! 66957 *Stephenson Locomotive Society 1909-2009* is about to be refuelled at Exeter depot, which is adjacent to St Davids station. Locos of any description are pretty rare here, but the presence of a Freightliner one is exceptional. The loco was in the area for route learning purposes, so an agreement must have been made between Great Western and Freightliner to allow the loco to use the facility. 6 October 2017.

Other books you might like:

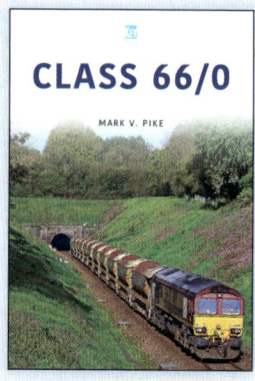

CLASS 66/0
MARK V. PIKE
Britain's Railways Series, Vol. 32

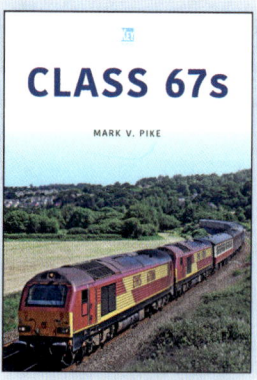

CLASS 67s
MARK V. PIKE
Britain's Railways Series, Vol. 30

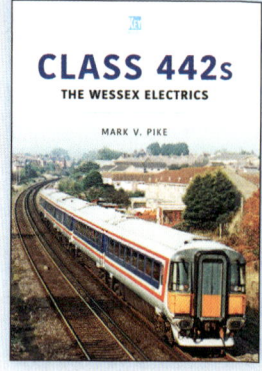

CLASS 442s
THE WESSEX ELECTRICS
MARK V. PIKE
Britain's Railways Series, Vol. 27

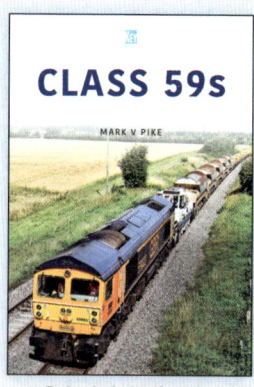

CLASS 59s
MARK V PIKE
Britain's Railways Series, Vol. 25

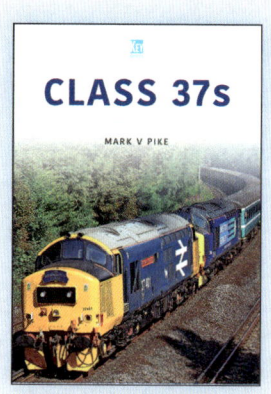

CLASS 37s
MARK V PIKE
Britain's Railways Series, Vol. 23

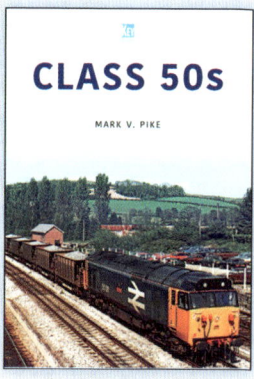

CLASS 50s
MARK V. PIKE
Britain's Railways Series, Vol. 36

For our full range of titles please visit:
shop.keypublishing.com/books

VIP Book Club

Sign up today and receive
TWO FREE E-BOOKS

Be the first to find out about our forthcoming book releases and receive exclusive offers.

Register now at **keypublishing.com/vip-book-club**

Our VIP Book Club is a 100% spam-free zone, and we will never share your email with anyone else. You can read our full privacy policy at: privacy.keypublishing.com